KETO DIET COOKBOOK

KETO DIET COOKBOOK

Simple Delicious Recipes
for
Weight Loss and Well-Being

3rd Edition

Jane Oliver

Contents

I am indebted to Jules Cann for her untiring help with this 3rd edition, particularly her assistance with all the new illustrations, recipe photos and layout.

Without her design know-how and formatting skills, it would have made the whole operation so much more challenging. Not forgetting her infectious enthusiasm….

Thank you!

Jane x

KETO
diet

salmon

berries

avocado

eggs

broccoli

nuts

olive oil

cheese

chicken

INTRODUCTION
What is a Keto Diet all about?

Essentially a Ketogenic (or Keto) Diet is a very low carbohydrate and high fat diet which shares similarities with the Atkins diet offering a very healthy alternative. Many studies have shown that a keto diet will help you lose weight, improve your confidence, increase your physical and mental well-being and may even help against cancer, Alzheimer's, diabetes and epilepsy.

Before going any further, let's take a look at the effect of carbs on your body. Your digestion system breaks down digestible carbs into sugar which enters your bloodstream. As this happens and your blood sugar levels rise, insulin is

1

produced and this prompts cells to absorb blood sugar for energy or storage. This produces sugar highs and lows associated with a high carb diet and an increase in weight.

When your diet consists of a reduced amount of carbs, the extra fat you are consuming along with the existing fat in your body are used to supply your body with energy. This metabolic state is called ketosis. Ketones or small fuel molecules are produced by your liver especially when blood sugar (glucose) is in short supply. These ketones serve the entire body with energy every day.

The aim of the keto diet is to eat around 20 grams of net carbs in your daily diet for highly effective weight loss and appetite suppression. Net carbs are total carbs less fibre and less sugar alcohols (if applicable). A good plan would be to keep to this strict diet until you reach your desired weight and then add a few more carbs to your diet if you wish to.

Each recipe in this book will show you the number of macronutrients. These make up the calorie content of the food. The three categories are carbohydrates, fats and proteins and the figures that appear above each recipe are per serving so you can monitor your intake. For clarity I have chosen to include net carbs in these figures.

What are the benefits of a Keto Diet?

Turning your body into a fat-burning machine will do wonders for your weight loss while keeping insulin, the fat storing hormone, under control. More than thirty high quality studies have shown that keto diets are more effective at weight loss than any other diets. Fat cells in your abdomen are normally those to get burned off first and used for energy when ketosis is reached and maintained.

It's fairly normal for those using a keto weight loss programme to find that feelings of hunger decrease hugely making it easier to eat at meal times without feeling the need to snack in between. Let's face it, most diets don't work because the hunger pangs become too much. Many people on keto diets find that eating twice a day becomes the norm.

It has been shown that a keto diet can keep Type 2 diabetes under control which makes perfect sense because blood sugar levels are now being maintained at low levels. Obviously for things to change, it means a lifestyle shift from the wrong type of foods to low carb alternatives where ketosis is being monitored and adhered to.

Since the start of the twentieth century, the ketogenic diet has been responsible for aiding people who suffer from epilepsy. In the early days it was children who benefited but such were the positive effects on epileptics that adults began to be treated too. It has been proven that those with epileptic tendencies who start a keto diet are able to do with less drugs or none at all with the possibility of remaining free from seizures altogether.

As the brain is now being fuelled 24/7 by ketones and not by the swings of glucose associated with sugars and high carb foods, many people have noticed a huge improvement in their mental performance. Indeed, some people embark on ketogenic diets purely to improve their mental performance. Positive changes in mental clarity, concentration and focus can often be traced back to changing over from normal foods to low carb ones. Ketosis supplies a steady flow of ketones (fuel) to the brain avoiding issues with large blood sugar swings.

A ketogenic diet ramps up your physical endurance as you access huge amounts of energy via your fat stores. When your body relies on stored carbohydrates (glycogen), these energy stores only last for hours of intense exercise at a time. Your fat stores, on the other hand, have enough energy to potentially last for weeks.

Typically, keto dieters confirm a pleasant and unexpected side effect of a ketogenic diet in that there is an absence of heartburn and reflux which can be traced to sugary foods such as chocolate and cakes. Improvements in IBS (Irritable Bowel Syndrome) symptoms can result when a calmer stomach means less cramps, a reduction in gas and less pain generally.

Lower blood pressure and increased levels of good cholesterol (HDL), can be attributed to a change to a low-carb diet. Even acne and migraines have seen improvements for some dieters.

So, in a nutshell, there is mounting evidence from many different quarters to attest to the efficacy of a ketogenic diet. It might not be the answer for everyone but a growing number of people are discovering for themselves the incredible benefits of this diet and for them there is no turning back.

Is a Keto Diet OK for everyone?

For the majority of people, a keto diet offers a really healthy, safe alternative. However, it is not recommended for women who are breastfeeding. If you're taking medication (injecting insulin) for Type 1 diabetes or if you are taking medication for high blood pressure, it's advisable to consult your doctor or dietician before embarking on a keto diet.

Food to Enjoy

The great news is that there is a lot of fabulous food allowable on a keto diet.

Vegetables: Generally speaking, vegetables that grow above ground have less carbs than those grown below like parsnips. Carrots, onions and beetroot are among the better root vegetables with lower carbs. Pretty much any green vegetables growing above ground are fine (including aubergines and tomatoes).

Dairy: High fat dairy is the norm. Butter, cream cheese, full fat Greek yogurt and double cream are fine. Be wary of full fat milk, semi-skimmed and skimmed as these contain milk sugar (lactose). When choosing alternatives like almond milk, choose only the unsweetened versions.

Meat: Poultry, beef, pork, lamb, game.

Eggs: All eggs are fine.

Fish and seafood: Any type is fine especially fatty fish such as salmon and mackerel.

Nuts: Some nuts are better than others with cashews being high on the carb list. Those with lower quantities include pecan, brazil and macadamia nuts.

Fruit: Strawberries, raspberries, blackberries are good berries but should be eaten in moderation as they all contain the fruit sugar fructose. Steer clear of most other fruits including raisins and dates. For example, a medium sized apple contains 20 grams of net carbs.

Drinks: Water is king when it comes to liquids. Other drinks low in carbs are: unsweetened tea (one sugar cube adds 4 grams of carbs), coffee, almond/soya milk.

Oils and sauces: Olive oil, coconut oil, avocado oil, mayonnaise, vinaigrette, guacamole, béarnaise, aioli, tabasco.

Flour: Almond and coconut flour.

Food that is off-limits

Sugar: Soft drinks, sweets, cakes, biscuits, ice cream, chocolate, jams, sports drinks, most fruit, orange juice, frappuccinos and any other high sugar coffees, energy drinks, non-keto milkshakes, beer, baked beans, sweetcorn, ketchup, BBQ sauce, maple syrup and other high sugar sauces.

Carbs: Bread, pasta, rice, potatoes, wheat, corn and rice flour.

Legumes: These include beans and lentils which are high in carbs.

Processed foods: Avoid convenience foods as they contain high amounts of carbs and/or sugar.

While these foods are not allowed on a keto diet, there are some great keto alternatives to discover like cauliflower rice to name just one.

KETO FOOD PYRAMID

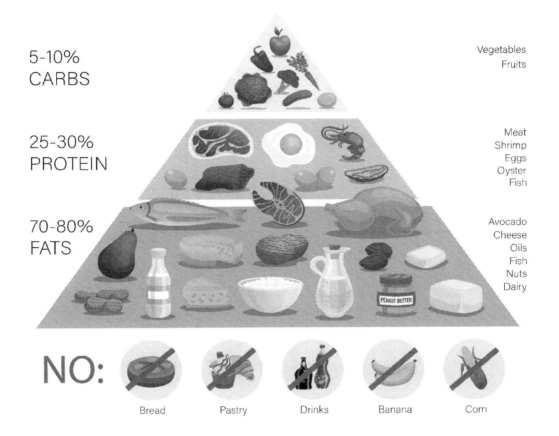

5-10%
CARBS

Vegetables
Fruits

25-30%
PROTEIN

Meat
Shrimp
Eggs
Oyster
Fish

70-80%
FATS

Avocado
Cheese
Oils
Fish
Nuts
Dairy

NO:

Bread   Pastry   Drinks   Banana   Corn

What if I feel like a snack?

Generally speaking, with a keto diet you will probably find you won't need to snack as much as you may be doing now but if you do, these will not upset your diet too much but remember that the following snacks will be adding carbs to your daily intake:

Cheese, a small handful of low-carb nuts and seeds, cold meat, hard boiled eggs, celery and other vegetable 'sticks' with guacamole/herbed sour cream/ cream cheese.

Is there any truth in something called Keto Flu?

When your body changes its metabolism from burning carbs (glucose) to fat and ketones, there is a chance you may experience some of the symptoms of what is commonly called keto flu. Not everyone who starts a keto diet ends up with these symptoms but it is just as well to be prepared.

Just to clarify, keto flu is not like a proper flu as we know it but you may feel a bit tired, nauseous and experience aches for the first few days. This is normal. One of the best ways to combat this initially is to reduce your carbs gradually over a couple of weeks. If you still want to go for the full keto diet straight away, then try drinking coffee without sugar to help with lethargy, and paracetamols for the aches. Also drink lots of water during this spell and add extra salt to your diet to counterbalance these side effects.

Sweetness and Light

Without sweeteners added to the dessert recipes, there is no way I could have included them in the scope of this book because the carb rating would be way over the top.

I've happily included two sugar substitutes that I've used in the recipes and they are all natural based. These are erythritol and stevia.

Erythritol is a low calorie sweetener, a sugar alcohol found naturally in certain fruits and is 70% as sweet as sugar. It doesn't spike blood sugar or insulin levels and has virtually no effect on cholesterol. The safety of erythritol has been endorsed by a number of studies.

Stevia is a popular low calorie sweetening agent. It's extracted from a plant named *Stevia rebaudiana* and the sweet compounds are found in stevia leaves. Stevia is extremely sweet (around 300 times sweeter than sugar) and, unlike erythritol, has been shown to have certain health benefits like lowering blood pressure in people with hypertension and lowering blood sugar levels in diabetics.

For Good Measure

A great deal of confusion surrounds food measurements around the world. For example, a tablespoon amount may have different connotations depending if you live in the US, the UK or Australia. It's fair to say that while spoon sizes do differ in the countries stated above, using the US measurement will not make too much of a difference to the overall recipe because we're generally dealing with smallish amounts. For simplicity's sake, you'll find US measurements appear first in the ingredients section followed in brackets by the metric equivalent.

In order to make the recipes understood for the maximum number of people, I've included explanations for some words (eg zucchini and courgette) that mean the same but are totally different words depending on where you reside.

The journey ahead........

One wise sage once said that a journey of a thousand miles starts with the first step. But before you take that step, it's advisable to know your 'WHY'. Why are you changing over to a low carb diet? Why is it important to you? What are you hoping to achieve? It may be to lose weight or for greater mental clarity or, indeed, for a greater sense of well-being generally. When you know why you are going ahead with this diet, place your answer on a Post-It and attach it to the fridge door so it's always there as a reminder. The reason is that the first week or so may be a little challenging for some people and this reminder will keep you going until you find you have settled in nicely to your new food regime.

Another useful tool to use when starting a new diet is to associate the feeling of pain with the foods that you've been used to and feelings of pleasure with the new low carb foods you'll be eating in the future. Start to associate pain with food like biscuits, cakes, ice cream, rice, potatoes etc. These are the sugary and high carb foods you've been used to eating and consuming. Change your thinking and see these foods as bringing pain into your life - the pain of putting on weight, mood swings associated with sugar rushes, brain 'fog', lack of mental clarity.

On the other hand, train your mind to view low carb foods as pleasurable, the ones your body needs and craves for - foods that will make you feel good about yourself as you lose weight, as you're able to concentrate far better and feeling good because you're actually sticking to something that's going to benefit you and your confidence levels. Add this exercise to your daily routine to help make the changeover easier.

My suggestion before you start the diet is to check your food stocks and remove any foods that you won't be able to eat while on this diet (check the list above and more comprehensive lists online). If you don't do this, then the foods you have which are not allowed may sway you off the diet and you may fall at the first hurdle. Any unopened packs that you don't now need can be donated to your local foodbank.

As with anything in life, you only get out of it what you put into it. My hope is that you'll make the change with ease and commit to this new healthier lifestyle and begin to see all the benefits available to you.

All that's left for me to say is that I sincerely hope that you love the recipes contained in this book and wish you every success with your keto diet. I'll be cheering you on all the way............

Jane x

11

BREAKFAST RECIPES

CHEESY MUSHROOM OMELETTE

Serves: 1

Nutrition per serving:
Carbs: 5g
Fat: 44g
Protein: 26g

Ingredients:

4 large mushrooms
3 eggs
¼ onion
1oz (30g) grated cheddar
1oz (30g) butter
Salt and pepper

Method:

1. Beat the eggs adding a pinch of salt and pepper to taste.
2. Cut up the mushrooms into bite sized pieces and finely chop the onion.
3. Melt the butter in a frying pan on a medium heat adding the mushrooms and onion stirring until tender.
4. Add the egg mixture.
5. As the omelette begins to firm up, sprinkle the cheese over the mixture.
6. Fold the omelette in half. When it turns a golden brown underneath, it's ready to serve.

Jane's Tips:

To make your eggs fluffier, make sure your eggs are at room temperature before cooking. Add a little bit of salt before whisking until they are frothy and light. You can add a little bit of cream for extra richness.

KETO SWEET PEPPER AND SAUSAGE

Serves: 4

Nutrition per serving:
Carbs: 5g
Fat: 13g
Protein: 26g

Ingredients:

10oz (280g) pork sausages*
1 large green sweet pepper
1 large red sweet pepper
½ cup (110g) grated mozzarella cheese
1½ tsp olive oil
All Purpose Seasoning mix
Black pepper to taste

Method:

1. Preheat oven to 450F (230C) Gas mark 8
2. Grease a medium sized baking dish
3. Slice off the stalk from one end of the peppers and remove the seeds. Cut into bite sized pieces and place into the baking dish, drizzle with 1 tsp oil, sprinkle with All Purpose Seasoning and black pepper. Place the dish into the oven and bake for 20 minutes.

4. While the peppers are cooking, pour the remainder of the olive oil into a frying pan, add the sausages and cook over a medium high heat for around 10-12 minutes turning often to ensure they're browned on all sides.
5. Remove the sausages and cut each one into four pieces.
6. Once the peppers have cooked, add the sausages and return to the oven for a further 5 minutes.
7. Remove from the oven and switch to a grill function. Sprinkle the cheese over the sausage/pepper mix and grill for around 1-2 minutes until the cheese has melted and has begun to turn brown.

5%CARBS **20%**PROTEIN **75%**FATS

JANE'S TIPS:

You can use sausages in a keto diet but check the product
1. is low in carbs (less than 2g per serving is best)
2. has no added sugar
3. is gluten-free ensuring high carb wheat is not used.

Look out for companies offering sugar-free sausages without dyes, nitrates, preservatives and other common additives often found in traditional processed sausages.

19

Jane Oliver

PULLED PORK BREAKFAST MIX

Serves: 2

Nutrition per serving:
Carbs: 11g
Fat: 21g
Protein: 16g

Ingredients:

3oz (85g) pulled pork
2 eggs
3 Brussels sprouts
2 tbsp chopped red onion
1 turnip
1 cup (60g) chopped kale leaves
2 tbsp butter
½ tsp paprika
¼ tsp salt
¼ tsp black pepper
¼ tsp garlic powder

Method:

1. Chop the turnip into small pieces.
2. Heat the oil in a frying pan on a medium heat and add the chopped onion, turnip and spices. Cook for around 5 minutes stirring every now and again.

3. Halve the Brussels sprouts and together with the chopped kale, add to the mix. Cook for another 3 minutes until they become tender.
4. Add the pork and cook for 2 minutes.
5. Clear two spaces in the mix and add the eggs, one in each space.
6. Cover and cook for 3-5 minutes until the eggs are done

BACON AND EGGS SURPRISE

Serves: 2

Nutrition per serving:
Carbs: 4g
Fat: 103g
Protein: 72g

Ingredients:

12 slices of bacon
6 large eggs
3.5oz (100g) full fat cream cheese
¼ tsp dried thyme

Method:

1. Preheat the oven to 200C (400F) Gas Mark 6
2. Mix the thyme with the cream cheese in a mixing bowl.
3. Hard boil the eggs, remove from the heat and peel them. Cut them lengthways and remove the yolks which you can set aside.
4. Fill the egg halves with the cream cheese mixture and place the halves back together again.
5. Wrap 2 rashers of bacon around each egg.
6. Place the eggs on a baking dish and cook for 30 minutes.

Jane's Tips:

The discarded yolks can be used by grating and using as a garnish on green vegetables or on top of salads. Alternatively, you could use them mixed with mayonnaise, relish, salt and pepper making a good spread.

SAUSAGE, EGG AND RADISH LAYERS

Serves: 1

Nutrition per serving:
Carbs: 4g
Fat: 49g
Protein: 32g

Ingredients:

7oz (200g) radishes
3.5oz (100g) sausages*
¼ cup (30g) grated cheddar cheese
1 large egg
1½ tsp olive oil
¼ tsp salt
¼ tsp black pepper

Method:

1. Fry the sausages in the olive oil in a pan for 10-12 minutes or until cooked right through and remove from the pan.
2. Chop up the radishes into small pieces and place in the same pan adding the seasoning to taste.
3. Cook the radishes for around 8-12 minutes or until they are tender.
4. When the radishes are nearly ready, fry the egg and put to one side.
5. Once the radishes are nice and tender, layer with the sausage meat, cheese and egg.

Jane's Tips:

Radishes are a great substitute for potatoes and 1 cup (116g) of raw radishes only contain 4g of carbs and are packed with valuable nutrients. Try roasting them in oil and spices for 45mins and they will surprise you with their mellowed flavour.

STRAWBERRY SMOOTHIE

Serves: 2

Nutrition per serving:
Carbs: 3g
Fat: 22g
Protein: 8g

Ingredients:

¾ cup (180g) unsweetened almond milk

⅓ cup (60g) frozen strawberries
¼ cup (60ml) heavy (double) cream
2oz (60g) cream cheese
½ cup (75g) ice
½ tsp vanilla extract
1-5 drops lemon extract

Method:

You can use raspberries or blueberries instead in this recipe but blueberries do carry a higher carb rating.   Mix all the ingredients in a blender until smooth.

TOFU BREAKFAST COMBO

Serves: 5

Nutrition per serving:
Carbs: 4
Fat: 11
Protein: 11

Ingredients:

14oz (400g) package of firm tofu
4 cherry tomatoes chopped
3oz (90g) cheddar cheese
3 tbsp avocado oil
2 tbsp finely chopped onion
1 cup (30g) baby spinach
½ tsp garlic powder
½ tsp turmeric
½ tsp salt

Method:

1. Take your package of tofu and cover in paper towels and carefully squeeze the water out.
2. Fry the chopped onion in $1/3$rd of the avocado oil until tender.
3. Place the tofu in the frying pan and crumble it down with a fork or masher.

4. Pour the remainder of the oil into the pan along with the garlic powder, turmeric and salt and gently stir the ingredients over a medium heat, stirring frequently to cook the tofu until most of the liquid has evaporated.
5. Fold in the chopped tomatoes, spinach and grated cheese and cook until the spinach turns dark green and the cheese has melted.

5%CARBS 20%PROTEIN 75%FATS

JANE'S TIPS:
Tofu:

There are several kinds available, each lending itself depending on the recipe.

1. Silken - sauces, batters, creams, dips, mousses.
2. Soft - scrambles and smoothies
3. Medium - soups
4. Firm - Stir fried and pan fried
5. Extra firm - All purpose

Jane Oliver

GOOD MORNING PANCAKES

Serves: 3

Nutrition per serving:
Carbs: 4g
Fat: 29g
Protein: 20g

Ingredients:

½ cup (50g) almond flour

4 eggs
4oz (115g) cream cheese
1 tsp lemon zest
Butter

Method:

1. Whisk the eggs in a bowl and mix together the almond flour, softened cream cheese and lemon zest until smooth.
2. In a frying pan over a medium heat, melt 1 tsp butter. Pour in 3 tablespoons of the mixture and cook for around 2 minutes until it turns a golden colour.
3. Turn it over and fry for an additional couple of minutes. Butter makes a good topping.

CHORIZO FRITTATA WITH SPINACH

Serves: 2

Nutrition per serving:
Carbs: 10
Fat: 110
Protein: 63

Ingredients:

5oz (150g) chorizo sliced
8 eggs

8oz (220g) baby spinach
5oz (150g) grated cheddar cheese
1 cup (240ml) double cream
2 tbsp butter
Salt and pepper

Method:

1. Preheat oven to 350F (180C) Gas mark 4
2. Melt the butter in a frying pan over a medium heat and add the sliced chorizo sausage. And fry until crispy.
3. Add the spinach and cook until it has turned dark green stirring now and again. Remove from the heat.
4. Whisk the eggs and double cream together. Pour the mixture into a greased baking dish. Top with the spinach and chorizo.
5. Add the cheese, covering the contents of the baking dish.
6. Bake for around 25 minutes or until golden brown on top.

Jane's Tips:

A frittata is a flat, firm Italian omelette which demands lower heat when cooking. Preferably use a cast-iron skillet, as this is non-stick and oven safe.
When cooked it should be yellow, not brown. To avoid browning, slide your frittata out of the skillet as soon as you remove from the oven. Use a salty, full-flavoured cheese for the best flavour. Remove whilst the eggs are still a little loose in the centre then sit at room temperature to avoid a rubbery texture.

LOW CARB PARMESAN TOMATOES

Serves: 2

Nutrition per serving:
Carbs: 3
Fat: 14
Protein: 17

Ingredients:

2 large beefsteak tomatoes
4oz (100g) grated Parmesan cheese
1 tbsp dried oregano
1 tbsp dried basil
2 tbsp fresh parsley chopped

Method:

1. Preheat the oven to 400F (200C) Gas Mark 6.
2. Grease a baking sheet
3. Slice the tomatoes into slices and arrange on the sheet.
4. Top each slice with grated Parmesan, basil and oregano
5. Bake for 10 minutes or until the cheese has melted. Top with parsley.

Jane's Tips:

The way to choose a good parmesan cheese is to look for one that has matured for at least 18 months and has a dry, crumbly texture with an uneven appearance.   Store wrapped in a layer of wax paper and then in foil in a refrigerator for up to four weeks. It can also be frozen for up to six months.

LUNCH RECIPES

ZUCCHINI NOODLES (COURGETTI) WITH PESTO

Serves: 4

Nutrition per serving:
Carbs: 7g
Fat: 22g
Protein: 3g

Ingredients:

4 zucchinis (courgettes)
1 cup (180g) of cherry tomatoes
½ cup (110g) pesto, green or avocado
½ tbsp of olive oil
¼ tsp salt
Pine nuts toasted optional

Method:

1. Prepare the courgettes into long, thin spaghetti-like strips using the spiralizer or by hand.
2. Add the oil to a frying pan and add the courgette strips. Fry over a medium heat for 3-4 minutes until almost tender.
3. Chop the tomatoes into quarters and add to the pan along with salt and the pesto of your choice.
4. Continue cooking for another 1-2 minutes. Top with toasted pine nuts.

Jane's Tips:

You can either buy zucchini noodles (courgetti) already packaged from your supermarket or you can make it yourself with a spiraliser or by hand.

There are two ways you can make this by hand.
1. A julienne peeler makes the job easier. Take the courgette and remove both ends. Then draw the peeler along the courgette to produce long, thin strips of the vegetable. Keep turning the courgette and stop before you get to the seeds in the middle.

2. The other way is to use a good old vegetable peeler which produces thick strips of courgette. Once you're done, stack the strips on top of each other and with a sharp knife, cut the wide strips into narrow ribbons.

EGG SALAD

Serves: 2

Nutrition per serving:
Carbs: 2g
Fat: 51g
Protein: 20g

Ingredients:

6 eggs
1 medium avocado
⅓ cup (75g) mayonnaise
1 tsp Dijon mustard
⅛ tsp dill
Small amount of lemon juice
Salt and pepper

Method:

1. Place the eggs in a saucepan and cover with cold water. Hard boil the eggs and when cool, peel them.
2. Chop the eggs into small pieces, sprinkle with salt and pepper and put to one side.
3. Mash the avocado adding salt and pepper to taste. Place this in a mixing bowl and add the mayo, eggs, mustard, dill and a small splash of lemon to prevent the avocado from browning.
4. Serve chilled.

KETO

5%CARBS **20%**PROTEIN **75%**FATS

JANE'S TIPS:

Hard boiled eggs:

Place in a pan of cold water, bring to boil. Turn off the heat straight away and leave covered for 10-15 minutes depending on the size of egg.

Run them under icy water and leave to cool for another 5 minutes.

Holding them in the icy water whilst peeling helps release the shell.

TUNA CELERY MIX

Serves: 2

Nutrition per serving:
Carbs: 4g
Fat: 28g
Protein: 13g

Ingredients:

2 tins x 6oz each (160g) of tuna chunks in brine
1 cup (100g) chopped celery
¼ cup (40g) chopped sweet onion
⅓ cup (75g) mayonnaise
2 tbsp chopped fresh parsley
1 tbsp lemon juice
1 tsp chopped fresh tarragon (or ¼ tsp dried tarragon)
½ tsp Dijon mustard
¼ tsp white pepper
Lettuce leaves

Method:

1. In a bowl mix the tuna, celery and onion.
2. Separately mix the mayo, parsley, lemon juice, tarragon, mustard and pepper and then add to the tuna mix.
3. Serve on lettuce leaves.

Jane's Tips:

Tuna is an excellent source of omega-3 fatty acids which are necessary for a healthy brain, heart and eye health. Studies show eating more omega-3 is associated with reduced rates of anxiety and depression as well as lower levels of cardiovascular disease.

For sustainable tuna look for the MSC label and cans labelled "pole and line caught". Also look for BPA-free cans. The most sustainable method of catching tuna is the pole and line method, which limit the impact of over-fishing. There are 7 varieties available to buy, but avoid the critically endangered species bluefin.

LEMON AND GARLIC ASPARAGUS

Serves: 4

Nutrition per serving:
Carbs: 5g
Fat: 4g
Protein: 2g

Ingredients:

1lb (450g) asparagus (½" thick)
4-5 lemon slices
2 garlic cloves
¼ tsp dried thyme
¼ tsp onion granules
1 tsp lemon zest
1 tbsp fresh lemon
1-2 tbsp grated parmesan cheese
Olive oil
Salt and pepper to taste

Method:

1. Preheat the oven to 425F (220C) Gas Mark 7.
2. Remove the woody ends of the asparagus and then wash and dry them.
3. Lay the asparagus spears on tin foil on a baking tray. Drizzle 1 tbsp olive oil over the vegetable and make sure each spear is coated.
4. Sprinkle thyme, onion granules, lemon zest, salt and pepper evenly over the asparagus and mix it in.
5. Top with the lemon slices and cook for 8 minutes.
6. While this is cooking, crush the garlic cloves in a garlic press and place in a bowl. Then add 1 tsp olive oil to the garlic and mix together.
7. Remove the baking tray from the oven after the 8 minutes and add the minced garlic evenly over the contents. Put the tray back into the oven for a further 3-4 minutes.
8. Remove the asparagus from the oven before it gets mushy. It needs to be bright green and not soft and bendy. Add the lemon juice over the asparagus and top with grated parmesan cheese.

Jane's Tips:

Asparagus is naturally cholesterol free and low in calories and fat. Your body needs cholesterol to build healthy cells, however high levels can increase your risk of heart disease and fatty deposits in your blood vessels.
Other nutritional benefits are that asparagus are a great source of vitamins A, C, riboflavin and thiamine as well as vitamin K which is important in blood clotting and bone building.

BEEF SALAD WITH CAPERS

Serves: 5

Nutrition per serving:
Carbs: 8
Fat: 3
Protein: 15

Ingredients:

1 large sized bag of green salad leaves such as rocket and mizuna
6oz (175g) cherry tomatoes
4-5 roasted red peppers from a jar
8-12 slices of cooked roast beef (depending on thickness)

The dressing:
2 tbsp lemon juice
1 tbsp wholegrain mustard
1 tbsp capers (chopped if large)
3 tbsp chopped parsley
5 tbsp olive oil
Salt and pepper to taste

Method:

1. Spread the tomatoes, red peppers and salad leaves on a serving plate and then place the beef slices over the top.

2. In a small bowl, place all the dressing ingredients along with some salt and pepper and whisk until it thickens. Pour over the beef salad.

SHRIMP AVOCADO SALAD

Serves: 2

Nutrition per serving:
Carbs: 7g
Fat: 33g
Proteins: 24g

Ingredients:

8oz (225g) shrimp
1 large avocado
1 small beefsteak tomato
⅓ cup (50g) feta cheese crumbled
1.5 tbsp chopped parsley
2 tbsp butter
1 tbsp lemon juice
1 tbsp olive oil
¼ tsp salt
¼ tsp black pepper

Method:

1. Peel the shrimp and de-vein if that's your preference. Pat them dry.
2. Melt some butter and pour into a bowl. Add the shrimp ensuring they are well coated in butter.
3. Heat a frying pan over a medium to high heat until hot. Add the shrimp to the pan searing for a minute or until they start to become pink round the edges, then flip and cook for a minute until the shrimp are cooked through.
4. Move the shrimp to a plate and let them cool off.
5. Dice and drain the tomatoes and dice the avocado placing them in a mixing bowl.
6. Add all the other ingredients to the bowl and mix. Add the shrimp and stir it all together.

Jane's Tips:

You can cook shrimp with or without the shell. The shrimp should be translucent and shiny with no odour. You can keep shrimp 3-4 days in the refrigerator and 3-6 months in the freezer. To prepare for cooking, remove the dark-coloured vein inside the shrimp and wash. When this flesh where the vein was removed turns from grey and translucent to pink and opaque, the shrimp is cooked.

CREAMY CHICKEN AND MUSHROOM

Serves: 4

Nutrition per serving:
Carbs: 4g
Fat: 29g
Protein: 27g

Ingredients:

1lb (450g) chicken breast
½lb (225g) mushrooms sliced
½ cup (120ml) chicken stock
½ cup (120ml) heavy (double) cream
¼ cup (60ml) sour cream
2 cloves garlic
2 tbsp butter
2 tbsp olive oil
2 tbsp fresh thyme leaves
1 tsp fresh parsley
Salt and pepper

Method:

1. Using a frying pan, heat half of the olive oil and half of the butter
2. Season the chicken and place in the pan on a medium to high heat until slightly browned on all sides. Remove from the pan and put to one side
3. Add the remainder of the butter and oil to the pan and cook the mushrooms until tender
4. Add garlic, chicken stock and herbs, scraping all the good stuff in the bottom of the pan.
5. Add the double cream and sour cream and simmer until the sauce starts to thicken ensuring the mixture does not boil.
6. Return the chicken breasts to the pan and mix into the sauce. Cook for 5 more minutes.

Jane's Tips:

Make your own keto chicken stock by combining a chicken carcass, onion, garlic, 3-4 litres of water, knob of ginger, parsley, thyme, peppercorns and bay leaves in a pot. Bring to the boil and then simmer for up 2 hours. Cool. Strain through a sieve. Remove any solidified fat off the top. Store for up to a week in the fridge or 3 months in the freezer.

CRAB AVOCADOS

Serves: 4

Nutrition per serving:
Carbs: 4g
Fat: 18g
Protein: 7g

Ingredients:

2 avocados
3.5oz (100g) white crabmeat
1 tsp Dijon mustard
2 tbsp olive oil
1 red chilli
Handful of fresh basil
Salt and pepper

Method:

1. Shred the basil and leave a few whole leaves to garnish.
2. Deseed and chop the chilli.
3. Break up the crab meat and place into a small bowl. Add the mustard, oil and salt and pepper to taste. Add the shredded basil and chilli to the crabmeat mix as you are about to serve.
4. Cut the avocados in half and remove the stone. Fill each cavity with a quarter of the crab mix using the smaller whole basil leaves as a garnish.

Jane's Tips:

An avocado will ripen at room temperature in 2-5 days, and can then be kept in a refrigerator for up to a week. The easiest way to tell if one is ready to eat is when it yields to gentle pressure and when you remove the stem, the flesh under the stem is a yellowish-brown colour. To prevent browning when the flesh becomes exposed to oxygen, dunk the halved avocados into boiling water for 10 seconds, then into icy water. They will keep for a few hours. However, to store for longer, tightly wrap in wax paper and store in an airtight container.

SMOKED TROUT AND BEETROOT SALAD

Serves: 4

Nutrition per serving:
Carbs: 4g
Fat: 42g
Protein: 16g

Ingredients:

2 x 5oz (135g) packs smoked trout fillets
9oz (250g) cooked beetroot
5oz (145g) bag watercress
1 tbsp creamed horseradish

Dressing:
3 tbsp vinegar
½ cup (150ml) olive oil
1 tbsp French mustard
Salt and pepper

Method:

1. Using a clean empty jam jar with a lid, place the oil, vinegar, mustard, two or three pinches of pepper and a pinch of salt. Shake and put it in the fridge where it will last a couple of weeks.
2. Remove the skin from the trout and break up the fish into bite sized pieces.
3. Remove any large stalks from the watercress.

4. Cut the beetroot into quarters and place in a bowl. Add the horseradish and 2 tbsp dressing and stir well. Mix the watercress into the beetroot mix.
5. Place the trout on top of the salad mix.

BACON AND CHEESE STUFFED MUSHROOMS

Serves: 4

Nutrition per stuffed mushroom
Carbs: 1g
Fat: 5g
Protein: 6g

Ingredients:

8oz (225g) bacon
12 medium sized mushrooms
⅘ cup (200g) cream cheese
3 tbsp chives finely chopped
1 tsp paprika
2 tbsp butter
Salt and pepper

Method:

1. Preheat the oven to 400F (200C) Gas Mark 6
2. Fry the bacon over a medium high heat until extremely crispy. When cooled, crush into crumbs.
3. Remove the stems from the mushrooms and cut them up finely. Fry them in the bacon fat adding the butter if needed.
4. Mix the bacon crumbs, and fried mushroom stems and the remaining ingredients.
5. Fill the mushrooms with the mixture and bake for 20 minutes until golden.

Jane's Tips:

The lowly mushroom is packed with essential vitamins and minerals and is an excellent addition to your diet. There are over 2000 varieties worldwide. But we are familiar with 5 common types:

1 - **Button** - Make perfect soups or sliced and eaten raw or fried.

2 - **Portobello** - Similar to button but much larger and perfect for serving stuffed.

3 - **Shiitake** holds an intense woody flavour. Perfect sliced thinly and scattered on salads.

4 - **Oyster** mushrooms have a delicate flavour and best seared quickly

5 - **Clamshells** come in white and brown varieties and are best cooked rather than eaten raw due to their bitter taste

AN EXCLUSIVE OFFER <u>ONLY</u> FOR

MY READERS!

As a Thank You for purchasing this book, I'd love to offer you a completely FREE book of tasty, new keto recipes and tips. Nine mouth-watering meals including Pork and Pepper Stir Fry, Yogurt and Lime Spicy Chicken and much more. Excite your taste buds!

Don't delay!

For your own personal copy, just use this link:

https://BookHip.com/GMSNKVW

Jane Oliver

DINNER RECIPES

LOW CARB SPINACH AND ARTICHOKE CHICKEN

Serves: 4

Nutrition per serving:
Carbs: 5g
Fat: 33g
Protein: 56g

Ingredients:

10oz (280g) frozen spinach
7oz (200g) tinned artichoke hearts
8oz (230g) chicken breasts
4oz (110g) cream cheese
½ cup (115g) grated mozzarella cheese
¼ cup (25g) grated Parmesan cheese
¼ cup (60g) mayonnaise
1 tbsp olive oil
½ tsp garlic powder
Salt and pepper to taste

Method:

1. Preheat oven to 375 degrees F (190 degrees C) Gas Mark 5
2. Cook the spinach and let it cool removing as much liquid as you can.
3. Drain and chop up the artichoke hearts, grate the parmesan and mozzarella cheeses.

4. Once cooled, place the spinach in a bowl and combine with the cream cheese, artichoke hearts, Parmesan cheese, mayonnaise, garlic powder and salt.
5. Pound chicken breasts so that they are an even thickness (around 1" thick). Season with salt and pepper on both sides.
6. Heat the olive oil in a large frying pan over a medium-high heat. Place the chicken breasts in the pan for 2-3 minutes to brown. Then place the chicken breasts in a large baking dish. Spread the spinach/artichoke mixture over the top.
7. Bake in the oven for around 20 minutes until the chicken pieces are no longer pink in the middle.
8. Place mozzarella cheese on top of the contents of the baking dish and return to the oven for a further 1-2 minutes until the cheese has melted.

CAULIFLOWER GRATIN

Serves: 6

Nutrition per serving:
Carbs: 6g
Fat: 23g
Protein: 14g

Ingredients:

1 medium cauliflower
1 cup (100g) grated cheddar cheese
3 tbsp grated Parmesan cheese
4 tbsp mayonnaise
4 tbsp sour cream
1 tbsp lemon juice
½ tsp Dijon mustard
Salt and black pepper to taste

Method:

1. Preheat oven to 375F (190C) Gas Mark 5
2. Slice cauliflower into bite sized pieces. Place the cauliflower into a saucepan, covering with water and boil for 10 minutes or until the cauliflower becomes tender. Then drain in a colander.
3. While the cauliflower is cooking, stir together the mayonnaise, sour cream, lemon juice, Dijon mustard and black pepper. Stir in finely grated cheddar.
4. Spray a baking dish with olive oil and then pour in the cauliflower pieces evenly. Spread the cheese mixture over the cauliflower. It's intended to just top the cauliflower not to cover it completely.
5. Sprinkle Parmesan cheese over the top and bake for 25-30 minutes or until the cauliflower is lightly browned

Jane's Tips:

For a bit of a variety replace half of the cauliflower with a head of broccoli and finish with sprinkled crispy fried bacon over the top.

KETO SPICY CHICKEN

Serves: 3

Nutrition per serving:
Carbs: 6
Fat: 17
Protein: 25

Ingredients:

1.5lbs (700g) chicken breast
4oz (110g) plain (natural) yogurt
2 tbsp garam masala
3 tsp fresh ginger grated
3 tsp garlic
1 tbsp coconut oil
Fresh coriander

Sauce:
14.5oz (400g) tin chopped tomatoes
½ cup (115ml) double cream
1 onion
2 tbsp ghee or butter
2 tsp fresh ginger grated
2 tsp garlic
1 tbsp ground coriander
½ tbsp. garam masala
2 tsp cumin
1 tsp chili powder
Salt

Method:

1. Cut chicken into 2" pieces and place into a large bowl with the garam masala, grated ginger, and minced garlic. Add the yogurt and mix. Chill for at least 30 minutes
2. To prepare the sauce, place the onion, ginger, garlic, tomatoes and spices in a blender until smooth. Put to one side.

3. Pour 1 tbsp olive oil in a large frying pan over a medium to high heat. Place the contents of the bowl into the pan to brown for 3-4 minutes per side. Then pour in the sauce and cook for a further 5-6 minutes
4. Stir in the double cream and ghee and continue to cook for another minute. Add salt to taste. Top with fresh coriander

CHEESY BRUSSELS SPROUTS

Serves: 8

Nutrition per serving:
Carbs: 8g
Fat: 51g
Protein: 24g

Ingredients:

2lbs (900g) Brussels sprouts
5oz (140g) bacon
1 cup (150g) diced onion
8oz (225g) grated smoked Gouda cheese
8oz (225g) grated mozzarella cheese
4oz (110g) crumbled feta cheese
1½ cups (360ml) heavy (double) cream
½ cup (120ml) sour cream
1 tsp garlic salt
3-4 tbsp olive oil
Black pepper and salt to taste

Method:

1. Wash the sprouts and then cut them in half
2. Heat olive oil in a large frying pan over a high heat. Once hot, take care as you place the sprouts in the pan and cook for 15 minutes stirring now and again ensuring they char a little on a couple of sides. Remove from the pan and put to one side.
3. Add the bacon to the pan, sauté for around 5 minutes, constantly stirring until the bacon is slightly crispy
4. Remove the bacon on to a plate with a paper towel base
5. Reduce heat to medium. Add the onion to the bacon fat in the pan. Sauté for 5 more minutes, stirring often or until the onions have become tender.
6. Add the double cream, sour cream, Gouda mozzarella and feta cheeses. Mix together. Reduce heat to medium-low once the cheese melts.
7. Transfer the Brussels sprouts back to the pan with the cheese sauce and mix. If the sauce becomes too thick, stir in some more cream little by little.

8. Season with garlic salt and black pepper to taste.
9. Garnish with the bacon.

Jane's Tips:

Other ideas for cheese to add extra flavours could be:

a. Gruyere – a good melting cheese gives a creamy, nutty flavour
b. Emmenthal – mild and buttery, a good melting cheese
c. Fontina – rich and creamy. Semi-hard with a taste of hazelnut
d. Havarti – soft and crumbly with a similar texture to mozzarella

Jane Oliver

SHEPHERDS PIE WITH CAULIFLOWER TOPPING

Serves: 5

Nutrition per serving:
Carbs: 10
Fat: 52
Protein: 40

Ingredients:

1lb (450g) minced beef
1 medium cauliflower
1½ cups (180g) grated cheddar
1 small onion chopped
1 medium carrot chopped
2 green (spring) onions thinly sliced
3 cloves garlic
4oz (110g) cream cheese
¼ cup (60ml) heavy (double) cream
½ cup (120ml) beef stock
1 tbsp tomato puree
1 tbsp olive oil
Black pepper
Salt

Method:

1. Preheat oven to 400F (200C) Gas Mark 6
2. Cut the cauliflower head into florets and add to a saucepan containing boiling salted water. Cook until tender in around 10 minutes. Drain and place into a dish lined with paper towels to remove any remaining liquid.
3. Return cauliflower to the saucepan and add the cream cheese. Using a potato masher, mash the cauliflower until smooth. Add the double cream, 1 cup (120g) cheddar and half the spring onions thinly sliced. Mix the ingredients together and season with salt and pepper.
4. Over a medium heat, heat the olive oil. Add the onion and carrots and cook for 5 minutes until soft. Add the garlic and cook for a further minute. Add the tomato puree and mix in with the other ingredients.
5. Add the mince to the pan, break up the meat using a wooden spoon and cook for around 6 minutes until it browns. Season with salt and pepper.
6. Add the broth and simmer for 2 minutes.
7. Transfer from the pan into an oven dish. Top with the cauliflower mash and then top with the remaining 60g cheddar. Bake for around 20 minutes until the top is golden and the cheese has melted. Garnish with the remaining spring onions

Jane's Tips:

It's worth the effort to make your own beef stock for the flavour and nutrients it gives you.

Start by roasting bones for an hour until browned. Then add these (including the juices) into a slow cooker along with a small carrot, celery, onion, tomato, bay leaves, thyme, parsley, coriander seeds, peppercorns and 3 litres of water. Cook on low for 8 hours. Strain, cool and once chilled remove excess fat. Store in a sealed jar in the refrigerator for 7 days or in the freezer for up to 3 months.

LOW CARB COCONUT CURRY CHICKEN

Serves: 6

Nutrition per serving:
Carbs: 6g
Fat: 17g
Protein: 14g

Ingredients:

1lb (450g) chicken breast
½ large onion chopped
14.5oz (400g) tin chopped tomatoes
7oz (200ml) coconut cream
¼ cup (60ml) chicken stock
4 cloves garlic
1½ tbsp. curry powder
1 tsp ground ginger
1 tsp paprika
2 tbsp olive oil

Method:

1. Place a frying pan over a medium heat and pour in 1 tbsp oil. Add the onion and sauté for around 8 minutes or until tender. When cooked, place the onion to one side.
2. Cut the chicken into bite sized pieces. Increase the heat to medium high. Add another 1 tbsp oil and the chicken pieces. Sauté for 1-2 minutes each side to brown.
3. Add the coconut cream to the chicken along with the tomatoes, chicken stock, garlic, curry powder, ginger, paprika and salt. Stir all the ingredients together.
4. Bring to the boil and then reduce the heat to simmer for 15-20 minutes until the chicken is cooked right through and the sauce thickens.

Jane's Tips:

See the recipe for Creamy Chicken and Mushroom for the method of cooking your own chicken stock.

LAMB SHANK HEAVEN

Serves: 6

Nutrition per serving:
Carbs: 6g
Fat: 59g
Protein: 57g

Ingredients:

6 lamb shanks
2 carrots chopped
2 stalks celery chopped
1 onion chopped
14.5oz (400g) tin chopped tomatoes
1 cup (240ml) red wine
1½ cups (360ml) chicken stock
1 tbsp dried oregano
1.5 tbsp rosemary
3 bay leaves
1 tbsp olive oil
2 tsp salt and pepper

Method:

1. In a large frying pan, heat the olive oil over a medium heat and brown the lamb on all sides seasoning with salt and pepper to taste. Once this has been done, place the lamb to one side.
2. Sauté the carrots, celery and onion for 5 minutes and then place them in a slow cooker.
3. Add the red wine to the frying pan and bring to the boil. Simmer for 1 minute and then add to the slow cooker.
4. Add the spices, tomatoes and chicken stock to the other ingredients in the slow cooker and mix together thoroughly.
5. Place the lamb shanks on top of the sauce and spoon the sauce over the top.
6. Cook on low for 8 hours.

Jane's Tips:

This is best prepared in the morning and placed into a slow cooker allowing 8 hours of cooking time. When cooking with wine, never add straight to a slow cooker as the lower temperatures don't allow for the alcohol to cook down and burn off. Always deglaze the pan with wine on the stovetop before adding to the slow cooker.

MINCED BEEF AND CABBAGE STIR FRY

Serves: 2

Nutrition per serving:
Carbs: 9g
Fat: 15g
Protein: 42g

Ingredients:

1lb (450g) of minced beef
9oz (250g) bag of coleslaw mix (green cabbage, purple cabbage, shredded carrots)
2 green (spring) onions thinly sliced
1 tbsp fresh grated ginger
2 tbsp soy sauce
1 tbsp sriracha
1 tbsp olive oil
Black sesame seeds

Method:

1. Combine the soy sauce and sriracha in a mixing bowl and stir until smooth.
2. Using a large frying pan, heat the oil and add the mince and cook for around 5 minutes stirring frequently until brown.
3. Add coleslaw mix to the pan and stir with the beef. Cook for around 5 minutes until the cabbage is tender stirring frequently

4. Reduce heat to medium low. Pour the sauce over the contents of the pan and add the ginger. Mix everything together. Add salt to taste.
5. Remove from the heat and stir in sliced spring onions and garnish with sesame seeds.

SALMON AND ASPARAGUS IN FOIL

Serves: 2

Nutrition per serving:
Carbs: 8
Fat: 19
Protein: 25

Ingredients:

2 salmon fillets
1lb (450g) medium thick asparagus
4 cloves garlic
2 tbsp vegetable stock
1½ tbsp lemon juice
1 tbsp sriracha
3-4 tbsp butter diced into small cubes
2 tbsp parsley
Salt and black pepper to taste

Method:

1. Preheat the oven to 425F (220C) Gas Mark 7
2. Cut 2 sheets of 14" x 12" (35 x 30cm) aluminium foil and lay each piece on your worktop.
3. In a small bowl combine the sauce ingredients – the vegetable stock, lemon juice and sriracha.
4. Season each side of the salmon with salt and pepper and then place on the foil in the centre.
5. Trim the woody ends of the stems of the asparagus and place the spears to one side of the salmon. You may want to blanch the asparagus in boiling water for 2 minutes and then drain before adding to the salmon especially if the asparagus spears are quite thick.
6. Mince the garlic and lay it over the contents of the two foil sheets and then pour the stock, lemon juice and sriracha over the salmon and asparagus.
7. Divide the butter pieces equally over the two salmon and asparagus.
8. Wrap the foil around the contents and crimp the edges lengthways and then the ends leaving a little extra space for the heat to circulate.

9. Place the foil sheets on a baking sheet, sealed side facing up and bake for 9-12 minutes until the salmon is cooked through.
10. Remove from the oven taking care as you unwrap the foil. Garnish with fresh parsley.

Jane's Tips:

Sriracha is a hot chilli sauce originating from Thailand. It is made of chilli peppers, sugar, garlic and vinegar and has a hot, tangy-sweet flavour. Use it like ketchup, on burgers, omelettes, stir-fries and add to sauces for an extra kick.

STEAK STUFFED PEPPERS

Serves: 4

Nutrition per serving:
Carbs: 7g
Fat: 45g
Protein: 34g

Ingredients:

12oz (340g) sirloin steak
5oz (140g) bell (sweet) peppers
5oz (140g) grated provolone (or cheddar)
4oz (110g) cream cheese
3oz (90g) mushrooms chopped
3oz (90g) onions chopped
1oz (30g) jalapeno
3 tbsp olive oil
1 tsp oregano

Method:

1. Preheat oven to 350F (180C) Gas Mark 4
2. Slice off the top of the sweet peppers near the stalk and remove the insides.
3. Place on a baking tray, spray with oil and place in the oven for 20 minutes.
4. Cut the steaks into strips. Heat up a frying pan to a medium high setting. Add half the oil and fry the onions until they're tender. Add the remaining oil,

steak, mushrooms and oregano. Cook until the steak is done depending on your preference.

5. To the cooked sweet peppers insert the steak and mushroom mix followed by the cream cheese. Top with more steak, jalapeno and provolone cheese.
6. Repeat for the other peppers and grill in the oven for 5 minutes so that the cheese melts.
7. Serve with a salad.

5%CARBS **20%**PROTEIN **75%**FATS

JANE'S TIPS:
Steak Stuffed Peppers:

Steak is one of the best sources of protein being rich in iron, zinc and magnesium. Peppers are rich in vitamins and antioxidants and therefore an excellent addition to a healthy diet.

This dish works equally well if made in advance and reheated the following day. You can also add in cauliflower rice to create more filling.

DESSERT RECIPES

CARROT CAKE GLOBES

Serves: 16

Nutrition per serving:
Carbs: 6g
Fat: 11g
Protein: 2g

Ingredients:

8oz (225g) cream cheese softened
1 cup (50g) grated carrots
1 cup (100g) shredded unsweetened coconut
¾ cup (80g) coconut flour
½ cup (60g) chopped pecans
1 tsp stevia
1 tsp cinnamon
½ tsp pure vanilla extract
¼ tsp ground nutmeg

Method:

1. Mix together the cream cheese, coconut flour, stevia, vanilla extract, cinnamon and nutmeg using a mixer.
2. Fold in the carrots and the pecans.
3. Roll the mixture into 16 balls and then immerse them in shredded coconut and serve.

Jane's Tips:

Stevia is a natural sweetener which has very low levels of carbs and so ideal for keto.
It is derived from the leaves of a herbal shrub native to South America, however most stevia food companies are using a chemically altered version. Alternatives are available such as erythritol, xylitol, yacon syrup and monk fruit sweetener.

STRAWBERRY AND RHUBARB CRUMBLE KETO-STYLE

Serves: 8

Nutrition per serving:
Carbs: 4g
Fat: 20.6g
Protein: 4.2g

Ingredients:

The filling mix:
1 cup (170g) finely chopped strawberries
1 cup (120g) finely diced rhubarb
1 tbsp lemon juice
1-2 tsp stevia/erythritol blend (depending on how sweet you like your dessert)
½ tsp xanthan gum

The crumble mix:
1 cup (120g) finely chopped walnuts
½ cup (60g) coconut flour
¼ cup (40g) flaxseed meal (ground flax seed)
¼ cup (50g) + 1 tsp stevia/erythritol blend
6 tbsp unsalted butter melted
¼ tsp sea salt

Method:

1. Preheat oven to 350F (180C) Gas mark 4. Mix the filling ingredients together. As you do so, sprinkle in the xanthan gum so it mixes evenly. Leave the bowl to one side.
2. In another bowl mix the walnuts, coconut flour, flaxseed meal, ¼ cup (50g) sweetener and sea salt.
3. Add the butter and combine until it becomes crumbly.
4. Measure out ½ of the crumble mix and add 1 tsp of the sweetener to it.
5. Grease a 9" pie dish with butter and line it with the mixture pressing down on to the bottom of the dish.
6. Pour the filling over the crust base.
7. Sprinkle the remaining ½ of the crumble mix over the filling.

8. Bake for 20 minutes covered in tin foil to prevent burning of the crumble topping. Remove the tin foil and bake for a further 10-20 minutes to brown the crumble topping.

AVOCADO BROWNIES

Serves: 12

Nutrition per serving:
Carbs: 2.8g
Fat: 14g
Protein: 4g

Ingredients:

1 cup (250g) avocado, mashed
¾ cup (75g) blanched almond flour
½ cup (90g) Lily's chocolate chips, melted
¼ cup (50g) erythritol
1 tsp stevia powder
2 eggs
4 tbsp cocoa powder
3 tbsp butter
1 tsp baking powder
½ tsp vanilla extract
¼ tsp baking soda
¼ tsp salt

Method:

1. Preheat the oven to 350F (180C) Gas mark 4
2. Mix the almond flour, baking soda, baking powder, salt, and sweeteners in a mixing bowl

3. Weigh out 9oz (250g) of peeled avocados. When mashed, this amount will equal 1 cup and then place them in a food processor and process until smooth ensuring there are no lumps.
4. Add the following ingredients one at a time to the bowl of the food processor – vanilla, butter, cocoa powder, eggs and melted chocolate chips.
5. Add the bowl of dry ingredients and mix well.
6. Place some parchment paper (greaseproof paper) in a 12" x 8" baking dish and pour the contents from the food processing bowl into it spooning the mixture evenly.
7. Bake for 30 minutes. The top should be soft when you touch it. Remove from the oven allow it to cool completely and then slice into 12 pieces.

5%CARBS 20%PROTEIN 75%FATS

JANE'S TIPS:

Keto-Friendly Flour

Almond Flour - Rich in natural vitamins and minerals . One serving gives just 6gms of carbs and 3gms of fibre. The flour is ground finely, although sifting will help the texture be even finer. Do this before measuring for a recipe.

Almond Meal - Having the same nutritional value to the flour, this is made from unpeeled almonds making it more grainy than the flour and better suited to making keto breads than cake baking.

117

PEPPERMINT MOCHA ICE CREAM

Serves: 6

Nutrition per serving:
Carbs: 4g
Fat: 38g
Protein: 6g

Ingredients:

2 cups (480ml) heavy (double) cream
6 large egg yolks
2oz (60g) sugar-free dark chocolate, chopped
2 tbsp instant coffee powder
⅔ cup (130g) powdered erythritol (or xylitol for a softer scoop)
2 tsp vanilla extract
½ tsp salt
1-2 drops peppermint extract
6 drops of stevia liquid sweetener

Method:

1. Heat the heavy (double) cream in a saucepan over a low heat stirring with a whisk.
2. Add the chocolate and keep stirring until it has melted. Add the egg yolks and continue stirring until just warmed.

3. Add the erythritol and coffee powder and whisk until it has dissolved completely. Continue to heat, whisking frequently until the mixture thickens in around 10 minutes.

4. Check the blend of ingredients in the saucepan by seeing if the mixture coats the back of a wooden spoon or by a food thermometer when it reaches 140F (60C). On no account allow the temperature to exceed 140F because the eggs will start cooking.

5. Stir in the vanilla extract, salt and peppermint. Refrigerate to cool.

6. When cool, churn the ice cream mix in an ice cream maker until it reaches the consistency that you prefer. Freeze any ice cream that's left over. If using erythritol, you'll need to allow the ice cream to thaw for around 10 minutes. If you use the sweetener xylitol, it keeps the ice cream softer so it can be easily scooped.

KETO APPLE PIE

Serves: 8

Nutrition per serving:
Carbs: 7g
Fat: 26g
Protein: 7g

Ingredients:

Pie Crust:
2 cups (200g) almond flour
6 tbsp butter
⅓ cup (70g) powdered erythritol
1 tsp ground cinnamon

Pie Filling:
3 cups (525g) thin sliced Granny Smith apples, peeled and cored
¼ cup (60g) butter
¼ cup (50g) powdered erythritol
½ tsp ground cinnamon
½ tsp lemon juice

Pie Topping:
1 tbsp powdered erythritol
¼ tsp ground cinnamon

Method:

1. Preheat the oven to 375F (190C) Gas mark 5. Place the melted butter, almond flour, sweetener and cinnamon into a mixing bowl. Mix all the ingredients well until crumbly.
2. Using a 10" springform pan, press the mixture into the bottom of the pan and about ½" high up the sides using your fingers or the back of a spoon. Bake for 5 minutes.
3. Now on to the filling. Mix the sliced apples and lemon juice in a bowl. Lay the apples in a regular pattern on the pie crust base pressing the apples lightly into the crust base.

4. Mix the butter, cinnamon and sweetener in a small bowl and microwave for 1 minute. Whisk until smooth and coat evenly over the apples.
5. Bake the pie for 30 minutes. Remove from the oven and gently press the apples down flat with a spatula or spoon.
6. Reduce the heat to 350F (180C) Gas mark 4 and bake for another 20 minutes.
7. For the topping, combine the cinnamon and sweetener and sprinkle over the top of the pie. Remove from the springform pan and slice.

PEANUT BUTTER BARS

Serves: 8

Nutrition per serving:
Carbs: 4g
Fat: 23g
Protein: 7g

Ingredients:

¾ cup (75g) almond flour
⅓ cup (70g) erythritol icing sugar substitute
½ cup (120g) creamy peanut butter
½ cup (90g) Lily's chocolate chips
2oz (60g) butter
1 tsp vanilla extract

Method:

1.   Combine all the ingredients (except the chocolate chips) together in a bowl and once they're all mixed well, add the mixture to a small 6" round pie dish. Spread the mixture evenly over the bottom of the dish.
2.   Melt the chocolate chips in a microwave for around 30 seconds and stir. Spread this over the mixture in the pie dish.
3.   Refrigerate for an hour or two allowing the contents to harden up. Cut into 8 pieces.

Jane's Tips:

As an alternative to almond flour, a mix of coconut and almond flour combined can work well together. The benefit of using coconut flour is that it is extremely high in fibre. Just 10 grams will provide around 10% of your recommended daily intake. Try a ratio of 3 parts almond flour to 1 part coconut flour. Mixing in strong flavours or spices can help to mask the distinct coconut flavours.

LOW CARB CHEESECAKE

Serves: 12

Nutrition per serving:
Carbs: 5g
Fat: 54g
Protein: 14g

Ingredients:

Cheesecake base:
1½ cups (150g) almond flour
⅓ cup (70g) powdered erythritol
6 tbsp butter, melted
1 tsp cinnamon

Cheesecake filling:
3lbs (1360g) full fat cream cheese
5 large eggs
8oz (225ml) sour cream
2⅔ cups (530g) of powdered erythritol
1 tbsp vanilla extract

Topping:
Add fruit of your choice. The topping needs to be added to the nutrition list above this recipe.

Method:

1. Preheat the oven to 325F (170C) Gas mark 3. Combine the almond flour, sweetener and cinnamon ingredients in a bowl. Mix the butter into the mixture. Empty this cheesecake base mix into a 10" x 4" springform pan pressing halfway up the sides with your fingers. Try using something like a flat-bottomed glass to press the mixture into place. Place in the fridge for 20 minutes.
2. To prepare the filling, use a hand mixer, beating the cream cheese until light and fluffy. Add the sweetener gradually to the mixture around ⅓rd at a time blending as you go with the hand mixer. In the same way, add the eggs individually and mix well. Then add the vanilla and sour cream ensuring the ingredients have all been mixed.
3. Pour the cheesecake filling on to the base crust. It doesn't matter if you fill it beyond the level of the base. Bake for around 50 minutes. If the top is still glossy, it needs a little longer.
4. Turn off the oven, open the door and leave it there for 30 minutes. Remove from the oven running a small, sharp knife round the edge of the pan to prevent sticking but do not remove from the springform pan. Cover with a food umbrella while it sits on your kitchen worktop for 1 hour.
5. Cover with plastic wrap (cling film) and refrigerate for at least 8 hours. Remove the springform pan sides and serve with a fruit topping.

Jane's Tips:

When making cheesecake it's important to have all your ingredients at room temperature before you begin. Any items that have been in the fridge should be left out in the kitchen for around 3 hours prior to preparing the cheesecake.

CHOCOLATE MOUSSE

Serves: 2

Nutrition per serving:
Carbs: 7g
Fat: 38g
Protein: 5g

Ingredients:

3oz (90g) cream cheese
½ cup (120ml) heavy (double) cream
⅓ cup (70g) erythritol
2 tbsp unsweetened cocoa
1 tsp vanilla extract
1 pinch table salt
¼ cup of blueberries

Method:

1. Place the cream cheese in a bowl and mix using a hand mixer until it becomes light and fluffy. Turn the hand mixer on to a lower setting and start to add the cream and vanilla extract.
2. Now add the sweetener, cocoa powder and salt mixing it well. On a higher speed, mix all the ingredients again for a further 1-2 minutes.
3. Sprinkle with the blueberries.
4. Serve immediately or refrigerate for later.

Jane's Tips:

Most fruits are too high in carbohydrates to be eaten regularly on a keto diet, but berries are the exception. Eaten fresh, strawberries, raspberries, blackberries as well as blueberries have lower carb levels and therefore are allowed. Dried berries, however would not be considered acceptable on a keto diet.

KENTUCKY BUTTER CAKE

Serves: 16

Nutrition per serving:
Carbs: 3
Fat: 27.1g
Protein: 7.3g

Ingredients:

Cake:
2½ cups (250g) almond flour
1 cup (225g) butter
1⅓ cups (270g) erythritol granulated
½ cup (120ml) whipping (double) cream
½ cup (120ml) water
¼ cup (30g) coconut flour
¼ cup (25g) unflavoured whey protein powder
5 large eggs
1 tbsp baking powder
2 tsp vanilla extract
½ tsp salt

Glaze:
⅓ cup (70g) + 2 tbsp erythritol granulated
5 tbsp butter
2 tbsp water
1 tsp vanilla extract

Method:

1. Preheat the oven to 325F (170C) Gas mark 3. Grease a bundt pan with butter and dust with a few tablespoons of almond flour.
2. Mix the almond and coconut flours, whey protein, baking powder and salt.
3. In another bowl, mix the butter and sweetener until creamy. Beat in the eggs and vanilla extract. Add the mixture from the other bowl along with the whipping (double) cream and water and mix until all the ingredients are well blended.
4. Pour the mixture into the bundt cake pan and smooth the top. Bake for 50-60 minutes until it has turned golden brown and firm to the touch. Insert a cake tester and if it comes out clean it's ready.
5. Now on to the butter glaze. Over a low heat, melt the butter and sweetener together. Whisk until they are well mixed before adding the water and vanilla extract.
6. When the cake is still warm and in the bundt pan, poke holes in it with a skewer and then pour the glaze over and allow it to cool. Using a knife or thin rubber spatula, run it around the pan to ease the cake away from the sides and then upend on to a serving plate. Dust with powdered erythritol sweetener.

KETO ORANGE AND CRANBERRY MUFFINS

Serves: 20

Nutrition per serving:
Carbs: 2g
Fat: 8g
Protein: 3g

Ingredients:

2 cups (200g) fresh cranberries
2 cups (400g) erythritol
1 cup (100g) almond flour
1 cup (280g) Greek yogurt
½ cup (60g) coconut flour
2 eggs
4oz (110g) butter
1 tsp baking powder
1 tsp orange extract

Method:

1. Preheat the oven to 350F (180C) Gas mark 4.
2. Mix all the ingredients, except the cranberries, into a bowl and mix well. Fold in the cranberries and then scoop the contents into 20 muffin cups.
3. Bake for 25-30 minutes until golden brown and firm to the touch.

Jane's Tips:

Cranberries - Fresh cranberries are made up of 87% water and fibres, and although a serving contains 9.2g net carbs, the huge nutritional benefits mean that including them in your keto lifestyle in moderation is important.

Fresh cranberries will keep in the refrigerator for a couple of weeks or so. But freezing them is very simple and they can be used straight from the freezer in a recipe without defrosting.

Spread out the sorted, washed, drained and dried cranberries. Place in a single layer on a tray and place uncovered in the top of the freezer for up to 5 hours. Transfer the frozen berries into bags or containers, seal and store for up to a year.

AN EXCLUSIVE OFFER <u>ONLY</u> FOR

MY READERS!

As a Thank You for purchasing this book, I'd love to offer you a completely FREE book of tasty, new keto recipes and tips. Nine mouth-watering meals including Pork and Pepper Stir Fry, Yogurt and Lime Spicy Chicken and much more. Excite your taste buds!

Don't delay!

For your own personal copy, just use this link:

https://BookHip.com/GMSNKVW

CONCLUSION

Thank you so much for downloading the Keto Diet Cookbook. I hope that this book helped you to get to grips with the Keto principles and that you are now enjoying these tasty low carb meals.

If you enjoyed this book, would you please do me one big favour and leave a review on Amazon? Your feedback and support would be really helpful as I endeavour to make this book even better and also, by sharing your views, it will enable others to benefit from the Keto Diet Cookbook too.

To leave a review, just visit your Amazon site, enter the name of this book in the search bar, click on the book cover, scroll down to 'Write a Customer Review' and leave your comment.

See below for quick links:

US Readers:
http://www.amazon.com/review/create-review?&asin=B087XD26SW

UK Readers:
http://www.amazon.co.uk/review/create-review?&asin=B087XD26SW

Thank you
Jane x

DO YOU LIKE READING BOOKS?
WOULD YOU LIKE US TO SEND YOU **FREE** E-BOOKS?

We would love you to join our Advance Readers Club.

All members receive free e-books on all sorts of interesting subjects which have included puppy care, cookbooks, joke books and mindfulness.

You will receive a copy prior to the book being published and marketed globally.

All we ask you to do is to read it and then leave an honest review on Amazon.

Please copy this link https://landing.mailerlite.com/webforms/landing/g7c3v6 into your search bar to be added to our VIP list of readers.

A selection of books from the same publisher:

For the full range, please visit
www.chascannco.com

HUMOUR

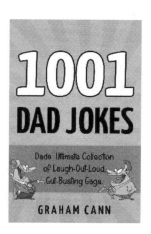

1001 Dad Jokes
Dads' ultimate collection of laugh-out-loud, gut-busting gags

SCAN THE QR CODE FOR YOUR COPY

COLOURING BOOKS

Fantasy and Mystical Art Therapy

Enter a world of fantasy and mysticism to help you relax, unwind and exercise your imagination

SCAN THE QR CODE FOR YOUR COPY

LIFESTYLE

Mindfulness for Beginners: A Practical Guide to Finding Peace and Happiness in an Anxious World
This easy-to-understand guide empowers you to take control of your life to bring peace and contentment

SCAN THE QR CODE FOR YOUR COPY

Made in the USA
Las Vegas, NV
03 March 2024

86646935R10087